W9-CSG-806

FIRE
FROM
HEAVEN

by Peter Youngren

ISBN 1-895-868-00-9

Published by: DOMINION MEDIA PRODUCTIONS
           310 Scott St., St. Catharines
           L2N 1J5

Cover design by Steve McLaughlin

Contents

1

BREAKTHROUGH IN BULGARIA

"Will this *'Jesus-energy'* work over the radio waves across Bulgaria?"

Mr. Roman had seen and heard a lot of things in his time. The well-known Bulgarian media personality had also interviewed many people on his popular radio program "Horizon." But this was another, different kind of horizon.

Earlier that evening, he and his staff were present at a miracle crusade in Central Square in Sofia, the capital of Bulgaria. They had recorded numerous testimonies of healings and broadcast them to a nation-wide radio audience estimated at twenty percent of the country's population.

My straightforward response on air, live, was: "Yes, but I will first have to spend some time teaching the Bible, God's Word, because that is how people will receive faith in their hearts to be healed." I continued, "Prayers are limited unless they are based on what God has already promised."

Meanwhile my mind was crowded with thoughts like, "Oh, God, help me! Give a noticeable demonstration of your power that no one can deny!"

Three days previously the crusade team and I had arrived in Bulgaria. We had heard that this was possibly the hardest nation of the former Communist bloc. Pastors told us to expect, at the most, 5,000 people to attend. Although we'd heard similar statements of caution many times, in our hearts we were believing God for 25,000.

Already, the first evening, our expectations were met, and God's blessings were evident. Blind eyes and deaf ears were opened, paralytics were walking, and there was a sense of something unusual in the air.

Ten months prior to our visit, it had still been illegal to mention the name of Jesus or quote a scripture verse in newspapers, or on radio or television. Bulgaria had been the most *Stalinistic* of all the Communist nations in Europe; even more so than Russia itself.

In December 1990, Central Square had been the focal point of mass demonstrations which had resulted in the overthrow of Communism. The government had reluctantly granted us permission to use the square, thinking that we would only need one small corner of it.

Several political parties had rallies scheduled simultaneously in other parts of the square. By the second evening the crowd had almost tripled to 70,000, attracting the attention of the media, including Mr. Roman.

The political party, that had scheduled their rally that night on the square, simply cancelled without protest since "it made no sense to hold a political rally when everybody wanted to hear about Jesus."

That night, on Mr. Roman's three hour program, God did something beyond expectation.

I had been told that the three hours were mine with the exception of a song that would be played every half hour. The special music would be by the "Rolling Stones" and "Aretha Franklin."

I couldn't help but laugh inside thinking, "Well, I've been in some churches where the praise and worship wasn't the best, but this really tops it all."

During the first hour, Mr. Roman asked questions like "Where does evil come from?" "Is there a personal devil?," "What's the difference between a *seance* and *healing through Jesus*?" "What is the Christian view of sex and marriage?"

The question, "Will this *Jesus energy* work all over Bulgaria?" opened the second hour of broadcasting. I instinctively remembered the instance when Jesus turned to the crippled man saying, "Your sins are forgiven you." The Scribes had been doubting Jesus' ability to forgive sin and it had prompted Jesus to further state, ***"That you may know that the Son of man has power on earth to forgive sins, I say to you, arise, take up your bed, and go your way to your house."[1]***

Certainly Jesus had validated the ministry of *salvation from sin* with visible healings. I knew He is *the same yesterday, today and forever* and yet, with everything within me, I was saying "God, please help me! Let Bulgaria know that You are real!"

After preaching and teaching for about 10 minutes and then praying for paralysed people over the radio, the power of God was so tangible in the studio that it prompted Mr. Roman to say, "There is such a *strong energy* in the studio that I think we have to take a five minute walk, and get some fresh air, or we'll all fall to the floor!"

We left the studio to the sounds of the Rolling Stones.

I've been to many charismatic services and seen people "slain" under the power of God, and here I was in one of the strongholds of atheistic Communism, the media headquarters that had propagated atheism for 45 years, and my host was worried he might be slain to the ground by some unknown power! I couldn't help but chuckle, thinking, "It sure is fun serving Jesus!"

We came back after five minutes and prayed for the blind and the deaf and all kinds of sicknesses, interspersed with teaching from God's Word to build the people's faith.

At the opening of the third hour of broadcasting, Mr. Roman said, "I want every person who has been healed supernaturally during this program to please call the station now. If you're sick, or have theological questions please do not call; only those who have already been healed."

I was nervous and excited at the same time. I looked at the one lone telephone in the studio and thought, "God, help us to get the right call through; anyone could tie up this line! Please Holy Spirit! Guide all those dialling the station from across the country!"

Within seconds the first caller was on the line. I anxiously awaited my interpreter's translation of the conversation. It was a *medical doctor*, who identified himself and stated, "I've been blind for 10 years. Just now I prayed with Mr. Youngren and Jesus completely healed me! I can see everything around me! This thing is real; it is not a fantasy!"

Well, we couldn't have received a better call! Here was a medical doctor testifying to the reality of Jesus! The calls kept on coming from people who had been healed attending the meetings in the Central Square, or while listening to the radio.

The media exposure kept increasing. It was unprecedented, especially considering that the mention of the name of Jesus had been banned for so long.

By the third night the crowd had increased to over 200,000 possibly the largest single Gospel meeting in European history. I always want to be conservative in estimating crowds. Sometimes ministers have been known to have a "gift of exaggeration!"

Well, exaggeration and lying are the same thing, but when I say 200,000 I am taking the lowest estimate. Many thought the crowd to be between 250,000 to 300,000, including police officers.

Bulgarian television provided 90 minutes *prime time* for an interview and, once again, asked questions about the Bible; about eternity; about forgiveness for sin; and healing for the body.

The Chief of Police commented that he had never seen crowds of this magnitude, not even during the overthrow of Communism. People from all walks of life - politicians, entertainers, as well as ordinary people flocked to the square night after night.

Half a mile from the square, police barricaded the streets, so that traffic wouldn't stop the people who were enroute to the crusade.

Some evenings there would be so many empty wheel chairs that it would be difficult to determine which chair belonged to whom. I would hold up an armful of crutches that had just been left on the platform, to show the people what Jesus was doing.

Once the service was over, some of the ushers from the local churches would walk across the square and find canes and crutches left on the ground, as people walked home healed by the power of Jesus.

I'll never forget the man who had been totally blind for 29 years; who could now see everything! Another man who came with a white cane and dark glasses, having been totally blind for 10 years, was seeing perfectly.

One of the most humorous healings was that of a woman in her 50's, who had a growth in her stomach larger then a basketball. Her neighbours surrounded her, crying and laughing, simultaneously telling the story of the size of the tumor. Well, during the mass prayer for the sick, the tumor had just fallen off and the woman had to quickly tie a knot in her skirt, to avoid losing it.

I've never seen people so packed together. It is a wonder that no one was hurt or trampled during that week of God's glory in Bulgaria.

Several charismatic and full Gospel churches were involved in the crusade, Pastor Krasimir, Pastor Hasabaranov and others worked night and day to answer phone calls, deal with the media and pray for people.

There were spontaneous outbursts of preaching and testifying in the city. One of our team members, Mikael Alfven, was surprised when he went to the bank and the post office to see people spontaneously stand up on a chair and start shouting to those waiting in the line-up (and believe me, people in the former Communist world are used to line-ups): "Come to Central Square; the blind are seeing, the lame are walking; Jesus is really alive! People if you don't believe me, come and see for yourself!"

These were unrehearsed street meetings; simply a reaction to the works of God that people were seeing.

During the radio program with Mr. Roman I was also asked to pray for the peace of Bulgaria. In a meeting with Mr. Roman eight months after the first interview, I was told that that prayer had been a "hit."

The Democratic Party, who narrowly won the national election over the rejuvenated Communist Party, had taken my prayer and made it a part of their radio commercials, playing it hundreds of times before the election.

Truly this is a new day in Eastern Europe.

In Acts 1:1 we read that Jesus' ministry is not finished; it continues. The accounts we find in the Gospels of Matthew, Mark, Luke and John are just the beginning of Jesus' ministry.

"The former account I made, O Theophilus, of all that Jesus began both to do and teach."

The very thing that attracted multitudes to Jesus' meetings 2,000 years ago in cities like Capernaum and Jerusalem, is still attracting and meeting the deep-seated spiritual needs of people. Everyone is created with a hunger for God that only Jesus can satisfy.

The ministry of signs and wonders is not for a select few, it is for every believer. It is a God given method whereby attention is focused on the name of Jesus and His saving power.

It is for you!

1   Mark 2:10-11

2

SORROW AND JOY

My life's calling did not start in July, 1990. That happened 17 years earlier, but the topic of this book started on July 30th, 1990.

I was in Stockholm, Sweden at Arlanda Airport with my wife, RoxAnne and our son Peter, one hour away from boarding a flight for Tallin, Estonia, now an independent nation, but at that time a Soviet republic. We were heading to the second largest city in Estonia, Tartu, with a population of one hundred and twenty five thousand people. This was to be my first visit inside what was then the Soviet Union.

Tartu was a forbidden city, so we had paid for five nights in a hotel in Tallin, although we would not stay at that hotel, but rather travel in our car to the city of Tartu, not yet open to foreigners. The hotel booking in Tallin was our "alibi" before the authorities.

Hours earlier I had received an urgent message to call my mother in Niagara Falls, Canada. I'll never forget standing by that pay phone at the Stockholm Airport and hearing my mother's voice on the other end, telling me that my father had just passed away. Just ten days earlier I'd been with my dad at the Niagara Falls General Hospital.

I said, "Mom, I'm coming home, I can't go to Estonia."

She responded characteristically, "You know what your dad would have wanted. We'll hold off the funeral for seven days. Your dad is in heaven and he would be very upset if you didn't finish the crusade planned in Tartu. I know the decision he wants you to make right now. You know how he has lived his life; nothing mattered to him more than world missions. So please go to Tartu!"

I knew my mother was right; I knew exactly what my dad was feeling in heaven at that moment. I could remember as a young boy, long before we immigrated to Canada, how he would receive newsletters from various missions organizations, outlining the prayer needs for various nations.

He would carefully study the need of each nation, praying earnestly for the salvation of people in Moslem, Hindu and Communist countries. He had been respected in the community where we lived in Sweden, and had an important position in export management. All his free time had been consumed by the work of God.

Often my mother and father would spend their weekends travelling to churches, as representatives of various missions programs, encouraging people to invest of their time and money, smuggling Bibles behind the Iron Curtain and helping the Underground Church.

I knew that dad had never charged a cent and had refused any reimbursement for travel expenses from the church he ministered in; meanwhile he and my mother had given as much as they possibly could into world missions. I knew my dad was with Jesus and he would want me to go.

We were taking a giant step of faith renting the football stadium in Tartu, probably being the first ministry to make such a move in what was then the Soviet Union.

Pastor Albert Turnpu from the Word of Life church in Tartu was to be my interpreter.

To our disappointment, the rain poured down in the afternoon and throughout the day when our first meeting was scheduled. At 7:00 p.m. when the first service was to start, the rain was still coming down.

To my amazement, two thousand five hundred Estonians stood at the stadium under umbrellas, waiting for the Word of God! When I gave the invitation to receive Christ, every single hand shot up in the air and everyone ran forward as close to the platform as they could and prayed with earnest the prayer of repentance and salvation.

The weather cleared up and by the fifth day, the largest crowd in Tartu history, over twenty-five thousand people filled the football stadium. What a sight it was to see the streets of Tartu jammed with people.

For two hours before the service it seemed that everybody in town was moving down the main street in one direction towards the stadium. After the meeting they were all moving in the opposite direction back to their homes again.

Every morning Pastor Albert Turnpu would greet me for breakfast with the statement, "I can't believe it. I think I'm dreaming. This is not really happening, is it?"

One visiting American pastor commented, "When I saw the thousands of people run forward to give their lives to Jesus it felt like a thousand volts of electricity went through my body. I could hardly believe what my eyes were seeing!"

Frankly, we had not expected this kind of success. We were ill-prepared. There was no follow-up material, no auditorium rented to conduct follow-up meetings. We had expected to possibly preach to a thousand or two thousand people in the largest service. All our expectations had been surpassed.

I had two thoughts racing through my mind simultaneously. One was a deceptive thought. "This is just a one time happening; this is what some would call a sovereign move of God, I just happened to be at the right place at the right time. This is a sovereign move of God, just for Tartu."

Then there was another thought, "God has a big plan for the Communist world. You must train up workers. This is just a beginning. Get ready for the biggest harvest of souls in the history of the Church. This is not a one-time thing." I knew this last thought was heaven speaking to me.

The experience in Tartu had also shown me another wonderful lesson. The style of preaching, the method of working that I had used for seventeen years in crusades primarily in India, but also in Africa and South America had worked also among Europeans.

Many of the people attending the crusade in Tartu Stadium were educated; doctors, professors, lawyers and economists. Tartu, after all, is a 350 year old city, built around two well known universities. In this centre of intellectualism, the same simple method of declaring the Gospel that we had used in the cities of India, had given tremendous results.

I simply preach the Gospel, invite people to receive Christ, pray for the sick and then take testimonies of instantaneous healings, which occur in the crowd during the message and prayer. This uncomplicated way of ministry had worked also in sophisticated, intellectual Tartu.

Some would say that such a simple approach would work only among people who already believe in the "spirit world" such as many of the tribal people in Africa or in Asia. Yet, in Tartu the blind saw, the deaf heard, the lame walked, and tumors vanished. It was evident by the pile of discarded crutches, canes, and wheelchairs that Jesus had been here, bringing great glory to His name. But this was just a beginning.

3

YOU SHALL RECEIVE POWER

To some North American Christians, terms like "miracles," "signs and wonders" and "healings" may appear suspicious. Charlatans have used trickery to counterfeit the true power of God for selfish manipulative purposes.

One must be careful not to allow this abuse by a few to become an argument against supernatural Christianity with "signs and wonders." Judas was a traitor, but all the disciples were not bad. Paul had a co-worker, Demas, who forsook him, but all of Paul's co-workers were not unreliable. One rotten apple does not make the whole bushel bad. We don't throw out the baby with the bath water.

The Bible clearly demonstrates that God heals sick bodies because He's compassionate, because good health is His will and because healing fulfils prophesy, just to mention a few of the many reasons.

Supernatural happenings, such as healings, publicize and create goodwill for the Gospel beyond anything that human marketing skills could accomplish.

"Then a great multitude followed Him, be-

cause they saw His signs which He performed
on those who were diseased."[1]

As a teenager, two writers made a profound impact on my life. One was Dr. Oswald J. Smith of People's Church in Toronto, whose vision for world missions has influenced my life for the past twenty-five years. His biography, "Not Made For Defeat" stirred my faith for revival in Canada like no other book has.

The second writer to have a profound influence on my life as a teenager was Dr. T.L. Osborn; especially his classic "Healing The Sick," which introduced me to the concept of "power evangelism."

At the age of nineteen I visited Trinidad and Tobago, in the Caribbean, to hold Gospel crusades. Knowing that there was a sizeable Hindu population in Trinidad, I felt I must prepare myself to present the Gospel to an audience of non-Christian background. How do you preach Jesus to people who do not believe that the Bible is God's Word and who are not used to our terminology or frame of reference?

To prepare myself for this task, I ordered ten cassette tapes of Dr. Osborn's preaching in non-Christian nations, eagerly anticipating to learn some "magic secret" to how Dr. Osborn ministered. I had read his books and seen reports of how people who had never held a Bible in their hand would be convinced of the reality of Jesus through a miracle.

As I listened to Dr. Osborn's cassettes, something happened deep inside of me. At first I was disappointed thinking that his voice was not nearly as booming and powerful as some of the Pentecostal preachers I had been exposed to. I thought his sermons were so simple. My logic could not reconcile how such simplicity could bring such amazing results.

I listened to the cassettes a second time, asking God, "Lord what makes this work?" I sensed a voice on the inside saying, "He believes what he says; that's the key!" Suddenly, something happened inside of me. Dr. Osborn declared, "Because Jesus is alive, tonight the blind will see, the lame will walk, the deaf will hear." And his words were not merely charismatic cliches. Dr. Osborn was not trying to get a polite charismatic response of "applause" or shouts of "hallelujah." The man actually believed what he said! I could hear the faith coming through in the words he spoke.

Something happened deep in my spirit, as I asked God to allow the gift of faith by the Holy Spirit to operate in my life in such a way that I would not merely speak religious sounding words, but that every word I communicated would be filled with faith, and *that faith* would become contagious in the hearts of the hearers.

For eighteen years now I've been able to see proof that such words spoken with the faith of God can cause years of scepticism against Christianity, years of Hindu or Islamic tradition or Atheistic thinking to be overpowered.

Simple faith in God's promises brings astounding re-sults.

In Pakistan tens of thousands of Moslems have gathered in cities like Peshawar, Karachi and Faisalabad. In India, a country known for large crowds, I have been told by ministe-rial fellowships in city after city, "Yes, we are used to large audiences meeting, but the unique aspect of this crusade ministry is that it gathers both Hindus and Moslems in unprecedented numbers."

Though we advertise to the best of our ability, the key to our success was never marketing skills, but simply presenting Jesus as a miracle working Savior, who is just as real today as when he walked the streets of Capernaum, Jericho and Jerusalem two thousand years ago.

The last two years have proven that it also works among sophisticated Europeans. I have never preached to people more open and hungry for the Gospel than the people of the former Communist world. Power evangelism works!

Philip practised it in Samaria.

> *"And the multitudes with one accord heeded the things spoken by Philip, hearing and seeing the miracles which he did."* [2]

Paul practised it in Corinth.

> *"And my speech and my preaching were not with persuasive words of human wisdom, but in demonstration of the Spirit and of power, that your faith should not be in the wisdom of men but in the power of God."* [3]

Jesus commanded us to practice "power evangelism." He said:

> *"Go into all the world and preach the Gospel to every creature. He who believes and is baptized will be saved; but he who does not believe will be condemned. And these signs*

will follow those who believe: In My name they will cast out demons; they will speak with new tongues; they will take up serpents; and if they drink anything deadly, it will by no means hurt them; they will lay hands on the sick, and they will recover."[4]

Power evangelism is not limited to a few select ministers. I tell people continuously, "If Peter Youngren, who is such an ordinary, average person can do it, you can probably do it even better!"

Hundreds of ordinary people from Canada, United States, and Scandanvian countries have taken their holidays with us to go on team missions ministry. While I preach evening crusades in the stadium, they conduct team ministry consisting of daytime mini-crusades at bus stands, market places, schools and villages.

One young farmer from Alberta, Canada, was preaching the Gospel along the Moslem coastlines of East Kenya. He was heckled by those standing by until a mother walked up with her son, a six year old boy, who was totally deaf. The young Canadian farmer laid his hands on the deaf boy's ears and they opened. The attitude changed; the heckling stopped; and everybody present wanted to give their life to Jesus.

Blind eyes have opened on the streets of Madras, Bophal and Bangelor, India. Miracles happen in cities like Sofia, Bulgaria; Prague, Czechoslovakia; Riga, Latvia; Novosibirsk, Siberia; and Alma-Ata, Kazakhstan.

Even shy, unassuming people who have never spoken in public before are experiencing the supernatural power of God as they minister. Seemingly untrained, ordinary believers are stepping out in faith, seeing wonders of Jesus performed before their very eyes.

Power evangelism is for you.

1   John 6:2
2   Acts 8:6
3   I Corinthians 2:4-5
4   Mark 16:15-18

4

FROM TORNADO TO TRIUMPH

Difficulties, confrontations, breakthrough. These words aptly describe what happened in Abakan, Siberia. It was as if the Kingdom of Hell was doing its level best to ensure that the name of Jesus would not be known.

I was in Abakan at the invitation of Pastor Rulsan Belosevich, a former gangster converted to faith in Christ. The second evening of the crusade was the most dramatic.

At 7:05 p.m. I was on the platform looking at the sun-lit faces of the choir members. The stadium was overcrowded. I remember smiling and thinking about how wonderful it was to preach the Gospel to so many people.

Within five minutes the sky turned ominously black, the wind picked up, and a tornado ripped through the stadium, throwing many of our more than forty large speakers to the ground. People scurried for cover, screaming in panic. The choir stopped singing. Confusion reigned everywhere.

When I stood to rebuke the tornado in the name of Jesus, the wind caught the heavy carpet on the platform, slamming it on my chest, almost knocking me to the floor.

With all the physical strength I could muster I remained standing, declaring the name of Jesus against Satan's kingdom, for this was obviously a direct assault from hell.

Within ten minutes the storm had settled and what had looked like certain defeat turned into victory. We had one of the most powerful healing services in memory!

There was such a manifestation of God's power that people were throwing their crutches and canes all over the stadium. Blind eyes were opened. We literally couldn't let everyone with a bonafide healing get to the platform to testify; there were just too many miracles.

A DROP IN THE BUCKET

It is impossible to adequately describe the spiritual hunger. Because of limited funds, we had only been able to bring 25,000 copies of a book for new converts entitled, "Welcome to God." Those 25,000 copies and 20,000 Gospels of John did not even last the first service. They were but "a drop in the bucket." Thousands were begging us for Bibles and Christian books.

Already the first night the all-time attendance record of the stadium was broken as 30,000 people packed the stands. The police were worried that the structure would collapse under the weight of humanity, so they ordered us to evacuate the top six rows. By the last night 48,000 people crowded into the stadium, filling the stands and field.

When the invitation was given to receive Christ, at least ninety five per cent of the audience would respond each night. Twenty thousand pre-printed decision cards were all used up the first night. It is impossible to know the exact number of people who received Jesus. We know that between 29,000 and 46,000 responded in each service, for salvation, but some may have responded several times.

At times like that, you don't worry about "numbers." Instead there is an awesome sense of ecstasy mixed with sobriety for God is shaking a city.

RUSSIAN POLICE

Two hundred and fifty police officers helped direct the crowd. They weren't exactly full of faith. The first night the chief of police said, "Don't worry if there are no miracles. We will protect you from the disappointed mob and get you out of the stadium alive."

Well, by the second night that concern was gone as it was evident to everyone that Jesus works miracles. The police were amazed at the attendance. No football or hockey game in the history of the city had ever attracted such a crowd.

The excitement did not go unnoticed in the city hospitals. Sick people were carried to the stadium in hospital beds. Hundreds testified of healings.

PARADE OF MIRACLES

Already on the first night people suffering from blindness and paralysis were healed. One lady had severe eczema on her arms and legs; people could see how her skin had been totally transformed.

Among the more notable healings on the second night — the night of the tornado — was a ten year old girl born deaf, who could hear and repeat the slightest whisper. One woman born totally blind received her sight. She was so overjoyed that it seemed like she would never stop kissing and hugging the people on the platform, while she was thanking Jesus for restoring her sight.

A man in his mid-forties, George Ivanovich, who had been unable to walk for eight years was running back and forth totally free. A lady in her mid-thirties came running with her crutches over her head, her legs totally healed after many years of paralysis.

A very happy mother came with her nine month old daughter, who was born blind and now had received sight. An eight year old girl, totally deaf, received her healing.

The miracles continued the third, fourth and fifth nights of the crusade, with a parade of testimonies. A young lady from Denmark, Berit, worked as our miracle recorder. She kept a running log, trying to get as much of the diagnosis as possible.

A PERSISTENT "GRANDMA"

On the Sunday night an elderly grandmother stopped me and would not let go, crying out for healing for her grandson, Patrick. She was so insistent that it reminded me of the woman in the Bible, who just wouldn't let Jesus go, until He had promised healing for her daughter.

> *And behold, a woman of Canaan came from that region and cried out to Him, saying, "Have mercy on me, O Lord, Son of David! My daughter is severely demon-possessed."*

But He answered her not a word. And His disciples came and urged Him, saying, "Send her away, for she cries out after us." But He answered and said, "I was not sent except to the lost sheep of the house of Israel." Then she came and worshiped Him, saying, "Lord, help me!" But He answered and said, "It is not good to take the children's bread and throw it to the little dogs." And she said, "Yes, Lord, yet even the little dogs eat the crumbs which fall from their masters' table." Then Jesus answered and said to her, "O woman, great is your faith! Let it be to you as you desire." And her daughter was healed from that very hour. [1]

The boy was born deaf and mute. Right in the throng of people, God's power touched the boy and he began to articulate words clearly. The next evening the boy and his grandmother told the story and the boy amazed the crowds by repeating sentence after sentence clearly in Russian. As I was whispering words behind him, his hearing was so strong, he could even mimic my accent of the Russian words!

The miracles brought a great sense of liberty. People who had previously been bound by the fear of Communism, applauded and sang with great joy.

TRIPLE HEALING

Nobody can forget the last night, when an eighty-four year old lady, who had been crippled on her right side from a stroke, and totally blind and deaf received her miracle. After testifying, she started to preach to the entire crowd saying, "Now is the time for the Soviet Union to turn to God." What a lady! She had survived Lenin, Stalin, Kruschev, Breshnev, Andropov and Chernenko, all the Communist leaders and now she was receiving Jesus.

It seemed that the healing power of God came in waves. Certain nights many crippled were healed; other nights there would be especially large numbers of deaf or mute healed. The last night there was a tremendous move of God among the blind.

I have preached in over 50 countries and we've seen larger crowds. Still, Abakan stands out in my mind. In African or Asian countries great miracles happen, but the minds of the people are often filled with so much man-made religious traditions.

In Russia the situation is totally different. It seems no one has religious opinions; there is a vacuum in the hearts and minds. How gratifying it is to preach the Gospel in its simplicity and power and fill that void with the reality of Jesus!

COUNTER ATTACKS

Anybody who has studied the Bible can very easily figure out that the devil was angry. It seemed everything that could go wrong went wrong. Not only the tornado, but for the first time in ten years, I did not arrive in time for the opening service! AEROFLOT had cancelled all the regular flights out of Moscow.

Associate evangelist Michael Alfven preached, and again,

God turned the problem into victory by demonstrating His ability to heal. It helped the people to realize the miracle power was not in one man; it was in Jesus.

The only adequate sound system available was owned by a Russian rock group. The first night the sound men got saved.

This was very much in God's perfect plan, because when the tornado struck it ripped the 380-volt cables. The sound men held the cables together with their bare hands as the police screamed, "Drop the cable or you will die..." With the sparks flying everywhere a sound technician responded, "We will not drop these cables; we must have sound so the people can hear about Jesus!"

The local Pastor, Ruslan Belosevich, a former notorious gangster had 3-4,000 attend his church every day during the week of follow-up meetings.

One month later the local medical association tried to discredit the miracles that had taken place. The local television station responded by doing a documentary. Rather than disproving the miracles, the television crew visited several homes in Abakan where people boldly testified that the miracles they had experienced in the stadium were lasting.

As we finished the Abakan crusade, which was our first endeavour right in the heart of Russia, I was overwhelmed with the openness of the people. May there be thousands of hearts set on fire! The potential in Russia is enormous. Let's do everything in our power to fill that inner void inside the Russian people. Only Jesus can satisfy that hunger.

1 Matthew 15:22-28

5

JESUS IS STRONGER THAN "NEW AGE"

My wife RoxAnne has her roots in Czechoslovakia. She describes the outreach into what some have called "the New Age capital of Eastern Europe" Prague, Czechoslovakia, like this:

"It was with special anticipation that I accompanied Peter to Czechoslovakia. This is the nation where my mother and my father were born. I was aware of a tremendous spiritual hunger.

"For several weeks up to the night before we were to start, the weather had been unseasonably cold and, had it continued, it would have made it almost impossible for us to conduct an open-air crusade. However, on the day that we were to start, the temperature dramatically increased and the sun began to shine. This continued until after our last meeting.

NEW AGE VS BIBLE CHRISTIANITY

"Signs of secular humanism and New Age philosophy were evident everywhere. A battle was raging for the souls of the people. Peter and I were impressed with how important it is that we reach the people now, rather than waiting for a more opportune time.

"One man, involved in 'New Age healing' using spirals and various apparatuses, said after attending a service where several paralysed people had been healed, "I am going home to burn all the equipment associated with my 'healing techniques' and I will not allow any more New Age healing services to be conducted in my home. I want to follow Jesus now.'

"Another man stood in the crowd, with his wife sitting in a wheelchair beside him. He got so caught up in the testimonies and the happenings that he forgot to pay attention to his wife. As the service was dismissed he finally returned to the wheelchair to bring her home, only to find the chair empty.

"People standing nearby informed him that his wife had simply walked out of the wheelchair, healed by the power of God. There was nothing left for him to do, but fold the chair and carry it home. His wife had already gone ahead.

"That same night another man was seen throwing his crutches out the window of a train. A local believer ran to pick them up, but the man responded, 'Oh, leave my crutches by the roadside. I don't need them; Jesus healed me!'

SIGNS AND WONDERS

"The list of miracles could go on and on as there was literally a parade of people each night, who had been healed of blindness, deafness, paralysis, cancer, tumors etc.

"It was the largest evangelical service ever in Czechoslovakia as crowds of up to 25,000 people attended. As in all these crusades, when an invitation to receive Christ was given at least ninety five per cent of the crowd would respond immediately. Pastor Alexander Fleck of the Water of Life Church is doing a tremendous work in Prague teaching and caring for the new believers.

"I brought so many memories home with me — the expressions of joy after a miracle had been received; the gratitude of the people; the tears streaming down a mother's face after her boy, born lame, rose up and walked — but most of all, the sea of hands raised as the invitation was given to repent and follow Christ."

So far RoxAnne.

On the heels of a tremendous victory in Czechoslovakia, we moved on to the Baltic republic of Latvia. Once again there was an opportunity for unprecedented spiritual advancement.

Local Pastors, never having been exposed to this type of a crusade, stretched their faith and were believing for 5,000 to attend.

However God had something far greater in store. On the very first night of the crusade 12,000 people crowded the crusade grounds, even though there had only been ten days to plan the event. By the final night 30,000 were in attendance. The 25,000 follow-up books for new converts did not even last two services. Night after night people responded. Many wept openly as they received Jesus as their personal Savior.

The Latvian people were awe-struck as the power of God began to touch people, causing miraculous healings to occur. Hundreds came forward each service to testify of God's miracle working power.

Blind eyes were opened and deaf people could now hear. Perhaps some of the greatest miracles occurred among the paralytics. As paralysis was rebuked, people, once crippled, began to make their way to the platform to testify about what Jesus had done. Empty wheelchairs and discarded crutches were brought to the platform.

One lady had a hip deformity and was unable to walk without the aid of crutches. Now she was running across the platform rejoicing at what Jesus had done for her. The expression of joy was priceless as an elderly lady, who had been confined to a wheelchair for four years walked and pushed her wheelchair across the platform.

An 11 year old girl named Sandee had been in a wheel-chair for six years. When I began to pray for the sick I noticed how she began to act her faith.

At first she stood up, slowly she started walking; then faster and faster. Eventually her mother brought her to the platform to show everyone what Jesus had done.

Elated with joy the mother recounted Sandee's story to everyone. After Sandee's empty wheelchair was brought to the platform, she pushed it back and forth, demonstrating her healing. Finally I sat in Sandee's wheelchair and she pushed me around in it. The crowd exploded with applause for the great work Jesus had done.

Few things, except salvation, are more thrilling than

seeing people come out of wheelchairs. In the area of praying for people suffering with severe paralysis, I have learned the importance of determined faith. In many of the crusades we would pray a special prayer for paralysed people, two or three nights in a row without seeing any result the among hopeless cases. Usually there will be manifestations of healing in people who have paralysis on one side from a stroke; or people walking with canes; people limping or who have had difficulty in movement; while the severe wheelchair cases, seemingly remain untouched.

More than once I've been in a crusade and after praying without any obvious results for several nights in a row, I've felt like quitting; like I'm making a fool of myself.

But what happened in Riga is typical of what I've seen time and again. On the fourth night of the crusade the first healing of a wheelchair bound crippled person occurred. It became a key to releasing faith in the lives of others.

This has happened in many places and has reinforced the lesson of faith time and time again. Do not look at the outward circumstances; keep believing what God's word has stated.

The manifestation of faith sometimes takes time, but with faith and patience we shall obtain the promise. As a believer I must fill my inner man with the promises of God's Word rather than with what the circumstances would tell me. If I start to look at the immediate results I may get discouraged, but if I look at God's promise, that promise will lift my faith.

Perseverance is a key to breakthrough.

6

SICKNESS COME OUT!

As reported by Norwegian journalist Petter Wilhelmson, editor of "Seierstro," a Norwegian interdenominational newspaper

By the tens of thousands, they flooded into Kazakhstan's biggest sports arena. "God created a perfect world but sin entered the human race and destroyed it," was the message proclaimed by evangelist Peter Youngren.

Close to 60,000 expectant people were pressed in to the stadium in order to hear about Jesus and in order to get healed.

He continued, "God could have turned His back on mankind, but instead He sent His only begotten Son to save you!" It was easy to sense the spiritual warfare raging for the souls of the thousands of people and for their future.

With an urgency, Peter Youngren asked, "How many of you want to turn from sin and live a new life with Jesus?" 60,000 people lifted their hands to receive Jesus as their personal Lord and Saviour.

The response was like an explosion in the realms of

darkness!

It seemed as if the enemy, Satan had been totally driven away, because everywhere in Alma Ata, a city with over one and a half million people, the talk of the town was about the healings, the signs and wonders and about Jesus and the events surrounding the crusade.

One of Peter's co-workers said, "Every time Peter speaks I feel like I want to get saved all over again!"

In an interview, Peter stated, "I know that God has given me the anointing to reach thousands of people and pull them into the Kingdom of God. It all depends on the anointing because it is the anointing that breaks the yoke. No words, no performance or personal charisma can do this."

JESUS LIVES!

It was with great expectation that I travelled to Kazakhstan's capital, Alma Ata, with Peter Youngren. After having been a part of these days, I can say with more boldness then ever before that Jesus lives today! He is a powerful and real Savior, who cares about all mankind: He forgives sins, saves and gives eternal life and He truly does heal from all sicknesses.

HEAVEN AND HELL

Peter Youngren does the work of an evangelist, but is also an uncompromising teacher, who declares the entire Gospel.

He preaches the truth; that which is needed so that people will turn from sin and have a chance to receive Jesus and have a personal relationship with Him. In order to illustrate this we quote one of the parts from one of his sermons in Alma Ata:

"God created a perfect world, without sin, without hate and without sickness. He created man in His image. Man was made to have fellowship with God, not to spend eternity in hell, but you were created to live in heaven. God did not create you to hate, but to love.

"God created legs not so that they would be lame, but so that you would walk and run. Just like birds are created to fly, your legs are made to walk. Just like fish are made to swim your ears are created to hear and your eyes are made to see.

"God created a perfect world, but listen people of Kazakhstan, something happened. Satan came on the scene. He tempted mankind. History's greatest tragedy happened. Mankind rejected God and sin became a part of humanity.

"Sin destroys because 'by one man sin came into the world and by sin came death, and now death has come to everyone, for everyone has sinned.' The results of sin are terrible; pain, loneliness, hate, demonic powers, hell, sickness, depression. Everything negative and destructive has its root in sin. The Bible says that 'all have sinned and fallen short of the glory of God' and 'the soul that sins it shall die.'

"How tragic! Listen! God could have turned His back on mankind and said, ' I won't forgive them, I'll leave them, because I told them not to sin.' But God instead so loved the world. He said, 'I want to bring mankind back into fellowship with me.'

"The question is how?

"God questioned, 'Is there one person on the whole earth without sin?' He searched, but in Asia, Europe, America, there was not one. In heaven there was one and only one; God's only begotten Son. His name was Jesus.

"God made a perfect world, sin destroyed it, but Jesus came and fixed it. He was wounded, beaten and hung on a cross to die.

"Why?

"The Bible says, 'He was wounded for our transgressions and He was bruised for our iniquities, the chastisement of our peace was laid upon Him, and by His stripes we were healed.'

"Jesus never sinned. He took our sin. Jesus was never sick, He took our sickness. Jesus died that we might be free. Jesus fixed it!

"You might say; 'well if Jesus took my sin, why am I still bound by it? If Jesus took my sicknesses, why am I still sick?' This is the case, because the devil has lied to you. But 'you shall know the truth and the truth shall set you free!' You don't need to go to hell. You can be free, free, free!

"You might say, 'well how can I receive this?' Turn around from sin and give your life to Jesus. How many of you want to do that today?"

EXPLOSION

An explosion of response resulted and it increased night

after night. Thousands of people wanted to get saved and hundreds of them wanted to testify of how Jesus had healed them from sickness. I personally saw how people's lives were changed as they were made whole. People hopelessly lame were carried in by friends, the blind, the deaf, people with cancer and different tumors all came looking for of a miracle.

A girl that was approximately 12 years old came on the platform together with her mother, testifying about how a tumor about the size of an egg completely disappeared from her throat.

A young boy had been lame for five years. The mother was ecstatic as she showed how she used to have to carry her son around. She'll never have to do that again because the son was completely healed. The mother recounted how the boy had told her "Let us go forward to the platform and tell Uncle Peter what has happened!"

This continued. One testimony after another about men and women, young and old, who had been healed. Some of them were so surprised and happy that they were left completely speechless. They just stood there on the platform and cried. There were many who did not receive the opportunity to testify of what had happened, because there was such a long line to get to the platform.

An older woman with crutches rejoiced over her healing. She carried her crutches over her head and began to run on her "new legs" for close to 10 minutes. As I saw her I was suddenly reminded of Peter Youngren's words just half an hour before, "God created a perfect world, your legs were created to walk and run."

SATANISTS

There was a tremendous openness for the Gospel in Alma Ata. All in all approximately 100,000 people responded to the call for salvation and thousands were healed. But along with these fantastic things, we were informed by the welcoming committee of something that awaited us at the next stop, Novosibirsk.

Two thousand Satanists had gathered there and were doing their Satanic rituals and proclaiming their curses with one goal in mind; to stop the crusades. But God gave the great victory in that Siberian city.

Anthony Greco, a 27 year old evangelist who has worked with Peter for five years, was to start the crusades in Novosibirsk. Already in the first meeting 35,000 people were present and many were saved and healed. I asked Greco what he had experienced or believed to be the most important thing in order to successfully reach a city:

"First and foremost, what happens in the crusade is the result of a personal relationship with Jesus. It is a result of a life, not of an event. In addition to this, obedience is very important. God must have one hundred percent of our loyalty and He must know that He can depend on us."

GRENADES IN INDIA

I spoke with one of Peter Youngren's co-workers,

Judy Hrabb, who frequently leads prayer teams in conjunction with crusades. I asked her about events that she particularly remembered from earlier crusades.

She answered, "India is always special, with much confrontation, but also great victory. Many people are saved and healed. I especially remember one incident which was very serious, where many hand grenades were thrown toward the platform.

"I thank Jesus that His blood protected us. Several exploded in the air and one under the platform. One also exploded in the crowd and it cost a woman her life. The crusade continued and tens of thousands were reached for the first time with the message of Jesus.

"During another crusade in India, there was a powerful storm. The sky was completely black and the clouds were thick over our heads. This almost destroyed our evening meeting, however we saw this as a direct attack of the devil against the plan of God and we began to fight against it in prayer.

"God answered us in an unusual manner and the people are still today talking about the miracle God did that day:

"All of a sudden, there was like a clearing in the sky and the light began to shine through. The clearing was right over the platform and it became bigger and bigger until the whole crusade grounds were covered.

"What was happening is that inside the arena there was no rain or storm, but outside there was rain and thunder. God is mighty!"

UNITY

After one of the Alma Ata meetings, two young men came on the bus. One of them wished to speak to Peter Youngren about a supposed revelation which he had received. In this revelation "God" had supposedly given him the idea for a flag that would illustrate the vision about "unity between religions." His main point was that it was Christianity that would bind all the other religions together. (The devil knew that if this lie was to reach people, then Christianity must be placed in the center.) So proudly he showed forth his flag, which had a cross in the center, which was to illustrate Christianity and on every other point of the cross there was a balance between all other religions such as Islam, Hinduism, Budism, and Judaism.

Peter Youngren responded, "This is a lie. There is only one name through which mankind can be saved and healed and that is the name of Jesus." The man became convicted, but did not want to turn from his ways. He left the bus saying, "I am sad that we can't understand each other."

A second man came on the bus. He had heard the previous discussion and wanted to tell how people had also been healed when he had laid his hands on them. Proudly he told of the power that he had in "his" village. He was the medicine man or the "healer" in Alma Ata. He seemed to be a little more careful in his statement than his friend, who had just disappeared.

"If your 'god' is so good, how come you see shadows that follow you and you are afraid to die?" Peter Youngren asked the second man.

This was obviously a word of knowledge, because it was noticeable to everyone around that the words hit him like a hammer.

With a scared and trembling voice he said, "How did you know that? Today I have hidden from shadows that follow me. I am always scared!"

The man was clearly under demonic influence. Peter Youngren told him about the fruits of the Spirit, love, joy and peace. He told the man that he needed to turn from sin, become born again and that he must turn around from the doctrines of demons.

We could see in his eyes that he hungered after God, but he still said, "Do I need to stop with what I'm doing today?"

"Yes you must and if you do we can pray for you now," Peter said. There was an obvious urgency in his heart for this man.

With a sorrowful voice the man said, "I must think about this. So much is at stake here." The man left the bus, but we prayed together that he would become born again and turn from his ways.

Truly, it was just like Bible days; some would rather hang on to sorcery than have Jesus in their life. This also showed me how "New Age" teaching has already gained ground in the former Communist world. The church of Jesus must not hold back. There is a spiritual war raging for the minds and hearts of millions.

REVIVAL

One of the bell boys in the hotel said with a heavy accent, "Can you pray for me?" He pointed to the place where he had pain. Everywhere we turned, there were people who had been touched by the wind of revival that was over Alma Ata. During one of our meals in the restaurant, one of the waitresses asked for prayer. Several of them wanted to be saved and healed.

There had been many reports on both local and national T.V. and the meetings were well known. Already the first evening there was an attendance record. Never before had so many people gathered together in a sports arena in Alma Ata. The National radio of Kazakhstan was on hand. Peter Youngren recorded sermons on five different subjects, that would be shown every day on T.V.

People just wanted to know more about the God who had done these things in Alma Ata.

The president of Kazakhstan also expressed his joy of what had happened during the crusade. One of Youngren's co-workers had spoken with the president, who seemed wide open to welcome Christianity to Kazakhstan.

Even if Islam doesn't have the same fundamentalistic influence as in Iraq or Iran, it is the most practised religion in the land; although it is to a certain degree, mixed with humanism and atheism.

In the midst of such circumstances the Gospel was touching lives like never before in history.

Almost all of these things can be summarized in one word. When there is a spiritual breakthrough on a level such as this, when an entire population is touched, it can only be described as one thing: "Revival."

7

FIRE FROM HEAVEN

It's 4:30 a.m. in Alma Ata and I can't sleep. There is a fire burning in my heart. I'm all alone asking God, "Lord, why can't I sleep? Speak inside my spirit?"

Unmistakably I hear His voice inside of me, "Make known what I'm doing, what's really happening in Eastern Europe. I want to use this story to set thousands of hearts on fire."

Alma Ata is the capital of one of the former Soviet republics, now a separate nation, Kazakhstan. The events of last night are still twirling in my mind.

58,500 individuals packed the National Stadium in our third meeting, in this nation that the Western media calls a Moslem state. The stadium has a maximum capacity of 42,000, but the stadium director allowed us to use the track and field areas as well as the large soccer field.

He basically had no choice, as the people were pressing in, refusing to be denied the opportunity of hearing the Gospel. The previous attendance record at any sports event was 30,000. That record was broken the first night of the crusade.

The reasons for the success defy logic. It's not promotion. It's not administrative skills — though we strive for excellence in all areas. It is simply an *anointing* from heaven. It's a *fire* from God. *Something* that God has put in our hearts attracts tens of thousands in city after city, nation after nation. There is no human explanation!

In one way, it seems we are not the right people for the task. My family and I already have a strong commitment in Canada. Less than two years ago together with forty believers, we started Word of Life Church in St. Catharines, Ontario. The church is only two years in existence and we are embarking on our first building program with a sanctuary for three thousand people.

It makes no sense. Why has God put us right in the middle of His harvest in Eastern Europe, while logic and common sense would indicate we ought to be focusing all of our energies on a building program, which in itself seems like a monumental task?

Sometimes I just chuckle and think to myself, "God, you're so good! I can't believe this is happening, but I'm enjoying it. Thank you very much!"

The local church is experiencing explosive growth while at the same time missions teams are being sent out. Isn't this what Jesus intended when He said:

> **"But you shall receive power when the Holy Spirit has come upon you; and you shall be witnesses to Me in Jerusalem, and in all Judea and Samaria, and to the end of the earth."[1]**

Many have interpreted this to mean "first" Jerusalem, "secondly" Judea, "thirdly" Samaria, etc. When we look a little closer at this scripture, it becomes clear that Jesus is not putting geographical areas in chronological order — rather he is speaking about a simultaneous outreach to Jerusalem and Judea and Samaria, etc.

Human logic and good intentions can never get this job done. It takes the fire of God. His word says, "He makes His servants a flame of fire."

Fire is contagious. Once you've caught it, you'll spread it.

Fire consumes. It burns to ashes that which hinders God's plans and purposes.

Fire catches your attention. Have you ever seen a crowd gathered around a burning house? There's something about the fire of God that so absorbs your attention, that other things seem insignificant and unimportant.

Fire purifies. It doesn't destroy gold, but rather makes it stronger. The fire of God makes your spirit man stronger, while it consumes things that are not conducive to a lifestyle dedicated to Jesus.

Fire changes landscapes, as is evident in many of the forest fires that burn down thousands of acres each summer in Northern Canada.

The fire from heaven changes the spiritual landscape from lethargy and lifeless churchianity, into vibrancy, energy, faith and whole heartedness. Visions and goals without the fire of God are just human planning and nice desires.

On the natural level one can plan a McDonald's hamburger franchise and might set goals as how to sell more hamburgers. While that kind of planning may work on a natural level, it will not work in the spiritual realm when you're up against powers and principalities and a host of wicked spirits.[2]

Only the fire of the Holy Spirit can generate the necessary energy that empowers a spiritual vision to break through into manifested reality.

The prophet Habakkuk wrote that a vision must be presented plainly *"that he may run who reads it."*[3] The time has come for the church to *run* with the vision.

There are two ways of running. One is on self-generated energy: hectic programs with a flurry of activities, which in the long run, are high on energy output and low on impact. Or secondly, on Holy Spirit-generated energy; fire from heaven clearly demonstrating God's miracle working power in healing the sick and liberating people bound by Satan.

Running with the fire of God is an antidote to boredom, misplaced priorities, selfish ambitions, burnout and disorderly living. God is looking for local churches that will have the vision, articulate it, and follow through on it in obedience.

Paul said, "I was not disobedient to the heavenly vision," indicating that it is possible to disobey God's vision for your life. Such disobedience leads to destruction as in the case of Judas Iscariot, the rich young ruler and a host of others. Obedience brings the blessings.

God wants *strong local churches that are obedient to his plan.* It is impossible to build such a church without a world vision. Canada and United States have yet to see what God can do through a local church, totally dedicated to Jesus and set on fire by God. Any local church that wants to sustain strength and growth must allow the fire of God to be the energizing force, as it embraces the world.

1   Acts 1:8
2   Eph. 6:10-12
3   Hab. 2:2

8

GIFTS OF HEALING

Physical healing is an integral part of the Gospel. Jesus spent approximately one third of His time healing the sick. Even a casual study of the Gospels of Matthew, Mark, Luke and John will impress the reader with the significance of healing.

Anyone believing in divine healing by faith in Jesus will meet opposition. This is nothing new. When Jesus healed the blind man, neither the neighbors, nor the scribes and pharisees were happy. Rather then rejoicing that the healing had taken place, they questioned "how," "why" and "what."[1] The servant is not above his master so we can expect similar opposition today.

There are different kinds of healings, the first one being the category I would call general healings. This would include viruses, germs or parasites which enter the body or bloodstream, as well as any body part not functioning properly. It would include general aches and pains and such things as problems with back, legs, arms or neck.

Another category of healing is the casting out of "spirits of infirmity." It is said concerning Jesus that *"He cast out the spirits with a word."*[2] Spirits of infirmity are demonic entities which can attack and oppress a certain body part. Demons are personalities without a body; for example a deaf spirit would control the auditory nerve, while a blind spirit might oppress the optical nerve.

A spirit of infirmity may control certain nerves in the body in such a way that paralysis is the result. Many of the healings we see is a direct result of commanding spirits of infirmity to leave in the name of Jesus.

As a matter of fact in each one of our services during the mass prayer, we would pray for blind, deaf and paralysed people by taking authority over spirits of infirmity.

When dealing with people whose sickness is caused by a spirit of infirmity, it is especially important that there is teaching and understanding of God's word, lest a worse thing comes upon them. In relationship to the man healed after 38 years of paralysis the Bible says:

> *"Afterward Jesus found him in the temple, and said to him, "See, you have been made well. Sin no more, lest a worse thing come upon you."* [3]

> *"When an unclean spirit goes out of a man, he goes through dry places, seeking rest; and finding none, he says, 'I will return to my house from which I came.' And when he comes, he finds it swept and put in order. Then he goes and takes with him seven other spirits more wicked than himself, and they enter and dwell there; and the last state of that man is worse than the first."* [4]

A third area of healing is "creative miracles." It is certainly a different kind of healing if for example, the nerves behind the eyeball is damaged as opposed to a person who has an empty eyesocket. In the latter case, a creative miracle would be needed.

One Russian lady had part of her finger amputated and while we prayed the mass prayer her finger grew out to normal size.

A Russian soldier sat among 38,000 others in our crusade in Minsk in July 1992. During World War II, while serving in the Russian army, in 1945, a hand grenade blew up by his ear destroying the inner ear and causing total loss of hearing. Forty seven years later his hearing was restored perfectly. It was a great testimony. This kind of miracle would be in the category of "creative miracles."

There are many ways that God brings healing to people, one of them simply being the release of God's power into a human body.

When the woman who had been sick for twelve years with the blood disease touched the hem of Jesus' garment, He responded *"Who touched me?"*[5] Jesus did not display a word of knowledge or a special revelation as to the woman's condition. He just knew that someone had touched Him in faith. This means that anyone in the crowd could have touched Jesus with the same faith because virtue came out of Him into the sick.

When we pray for the sick with the laying on of hands, we often "pray in tongues" or "pray in the Spirit." We may not know every detail of a person's condition, but we can be assured the Holy Spirit does and so when we lay hands on them and pray, we believe the virtue of Jesus is administered. Jesus, after all was the one who commissioned us to "lay hands on the sick."

In this type of healing there are two determining factors. First, the degree of the power of God administered into a sick body. Secondly, the degree of faith which activates the healing power administrated.

When Jesus came to Nazareth *"He could do no mighty work"* and *"marvelled at their unbelief."*[6] On the other hand in Capernaum "all" who came to Him were healed. Jesus had the same power operating in His life in both cities, but in Nazareth there was not the same degree of faith to activate the healing power of God.

There is always a requirement of cooperation from the sick person. That's why Jesus said things like, "Arise, take your bed," "Your faith has made you whole," "do you believe?" or "stretch forth your hand."

Jesus was looking for faith. This kind of cooperation in faith is very important.

In May 1992 when we visited six cities in Bulgaria, God did remarkable things. The first night in the city of Plovdiv, in spite of pouring rain, forty thousand people waited at the Central Square to hear God's word.

One of them was a mother with her five year old son, Vasco, who was born crippled. Well his mother was so desirous of a miracle that nothing was going to deter her, certainly not bad weather. In anticipation of the miracle she had purchased Vasco a new suit and brand new shoes.

Now logic tells us that a boy, who cannot walk does not need shoes. However the mother's faith in God's willingness and ability to heal overcame the circumstances. As an act of faith she purchased the shoes.

What a tremendous time in the service as Vasco rose up and walked. I remember him vividly, walking back and forth on the platform, grinning from ear to ear while his mother was crying tears of joy.

By the second day in Plovdiv, the crowd had increased to seventy thousand. The healing of Vasco is a great example of faith activating the power of God.

Healing also comes through spoken faith words. Actually prayer is rare in reference to healing. Jesus prayed outside Lazarus' tomb, but He states that it is more of a prayer for the sake of the people standing by. In James 5:16 we are told to *"Confess your faults one to another and pray for one another that you may be healed."* Certainly it is correct and biblical to pray for the sick, however to speak faith words is more common in the Bible. Jesus spoke to people, *"Rise up and walk." "Be cleansed from leprosy." "Go your way, your son lives,"* etc. *"He sent His word and healed them."* [7]

When I minister in mass crusades this is the method that God leads us to use more than any other. I simply speak words of faith to all those gathered. This is not like a lecture in chemistry, physics or biology. Rather the word of God contains in itself power.

When that word is believed and acted upon it brings tremendous results and you can actually see hundreds of people being simultaneously healed in various parts of a stadium or in a city square, wherever the meeting is conducted.

1   John 9
2   Matthew 8:16
3   John 5:14
4   Luke 11:24-26
5   Mark 5:30
6   Mark 5:5,6
7   Psalm 107:20

9

MIRACLE EXPLOSION IN A NUCLEAR ZONE!

It doesn't take a great mind to comprehend that one person can never get the job of world of evangelism done. It takes the whole body of Christ. For years I've had a longing to raise up others, who will understand the simple method of preaching faith in Jesus, helping crowds of people to receive faith in their heart.

A father may not rejoice when one of his friends have greater success then he, yet if one of his children does, a real father will be happy. This is the kind of *fatherly leadership* needed in the church of Jesus Christ.

I've asked God to help me to exercise this kind of leadership among the associate ministers that work within our organization. It brings me great joy when I hear the reports of what God has done and how God has used them to shake cities and see stadiums filled with people hungry for the reality of God.

One of those associates is Anthony Greco. Here he tells the story of a miracle explosion in the Russian nuclear polygon:

"Semipalatinsk has been a "closed" city. For several years the Soviet military detonated nuclear weapons only 180 kilometres from this city in Kazakhstan.

"When I approached the Mayor he gladly provided an official letter of invitation to conduct a crusade in the 10,000 seat stadium, which he provided free of charge.

"Unable to find any evangelical believers in this city, the crusade was organized in partnership with the New Life Church in Alma Ata several hundred miles away. A team of 26 people joined forces with us to penetrate this region and establish a new work.

"The first night, we were scrutinized by 8,000 extremely silent spectators. Even as the New Life worship team rejoiced during the praise and worship time, there was no response from the crowd.

"To complicate the situation, the people remained at the farthest possible distance from the platform. They seemed distant in spirit and body. However, when the call for repentance was given, over 7,000 stood to their feet! It was beyond expectation!

"The first healing miracle was not only dramatic, but visible to the entire stadium. Seated at the far end of the field, Valentina, a middle-aged woman, born with club feet, threw her canes and began to walk. Instantly her feet were turned to the normal position! Tears were streaming down her face as she walked across the field, stopping every ten metres to fall on her knees and lift her hands in worship to Jesus. The crowd was stunned for several minutes and then erupted in shouts!

"Soon many began to testify of miracles. A young boy

deafened in a car accident six years earlier, wept with his mother in gratitude over God's goodness for opening his ears.

"Another lady, paralysed for eight years down one side of her body, gallantly marched, jumped and waved her arms demonstrating her healing.

"Larisa, had been operated on for cancer, and then more tumors were found. Cancelling her operation, she travelled over 350 kilometres to attend the services. She came with great pain and swelling, unable to walk. She shouted and danced on the platform as the pain, tumors and swelling had instantly vanished.

"The second night the stadium was almost full. Already people began to show signs of change. They clapped to the music and even interrupted the preaching with applause on numerous occasions. It was evident that the Gospel was penetrating the hearts of people and breaking the cold spiritual climate.

"Many testified of healings. An old Kazakh couple with their middle-aged daughter laughed together, as the parents testified of Jesus' healing power. The father and mother had been paralysed by strokes. The mother had been unable to walk and the father was paralysed down his right side.

"Asiel, an eight year old girl, who had not walked since she was two years old, was wonderfully healed, prancing on the platform to cheers of the multitudes.

"Maybe the most touching miracle was a young couple, who for over 20 minutes sobbed uncontrollably in each others arms. After regaining their composure, the husband, Vassio, shared that since an accident two years ago, he had lost his speech and memory. I asked him what his address was and he responded clearly, stating where he lived. His wife was amazed, and with tears she said, 'He could not do that before'!

"Known as the main city of the nuclear polygon, fear of cancer and radiation sickness was rampant. Geiger counters were publicly displayed throughout the city to ease public concern. The reality of cancer was a nightmare come true for many in this city. Often the wind would carry the radiation from a nuclear explosion over the surrounding villages and towns. It was no wonder that the last night we had an explosion of our own of God's miracle power as hundreds were healed of tumors and cancer.

"It is difficult to accurately portray the final service. When one understands the depression, and fear of the people, the implication of this outreach is mind staggering. The attendance record of the stadium was shattered, as 17,000 crowded together.

"A floodgate of healing testimonies broke forth. Within the first twenty testimonies, fifteen individuals had been healed of tumors. Many had multiple growths, one even the size of a large grapefruit.

"It seemed that the entire crowd stood to their feet to receive Jesus. As the service concluded, no one wanted to leave. The people lifted their hands and joined the New Life worship group in praising God, for almost an hour after the close.

"The follow-up services were beyond expectation as well. On the third night over three hundred received the Holy Spirit and began to speak in tongues. Today the Church is alive in Semipalatinsk with hundreds of believers."

FIRST STADIUM CRUSADE HELD IN THE SOVIET UNION!!!

In June 1990, when Perestroyka and Glasnost were only beginning we launched a crusade into an atheistic stronghold of the Soviet Union. Tartu, Estonia was the site of that histroic meeting; the first mass open air crusade in the history of the U.S.S.R.

Above: An aerial shot of the stadium during the first open air crusade in Siberia. We had to evacuate the top six rows because police thought the structure would collapse under the weight of humanity.

Left: This man's crippled legs were miraculously healed by Jesus. Here we see him running across the platform.

Right: In order to demonstrate a healing from blindness, I ask this woman to grab my nose while I keep moving my head from side to side. This lady was also healed of deafness and paralysis on the left side from a stroke.

ABAKAN, SIBERIA

Right: With crutches held high, this young man runs back and forth across the platform declaring to the crowd gathered that Jesus healed his crippled legs.

Below: As the call for salvation is given, a sea of hands are raised to receive Jesus. More than 24,000 people were present during this meeting.

PRAGUE, CZECHOSLOVAKIA

Above: A section of the crowd from Riga, Latvia.

Above: This woman, healed of paraylisis, holds her crutches high to celebrate the triumph of the miracle working power of Jesus.

Left: Word of Life Church team member Alvin Esau holds a discarded wheelchair for the crowd to see.

RIGA, LATVIA

MORE THAN 200,000 PEOPLE GATHERED AT CENTRAL SQUARE IN SOFIA, BULGARIA

SOFIA, BULGARIA

Left: Peter holds up crutches that had been discarded by people who were healed.

Below: A man comes forward to testify after Jesus opened his eyes which had been blind for ten years.

Bottom: An aerial view of the crowd in Central Square

SOFIA, BULGARIA

Above Left: This World War II veteran lost his hearing when a grenade exploded near his ear. Here he demonstrates his healing.
Above Right: A woman healed of paralysis.
Right: This little girl was crippled but now walks.

MINSK, RUSSIA

Reis and JoAnn James conducted our outreach into Ufa, Bellorussia.
On the left we see Reis preaching to 40,000 people.
Below, Joanne distributes follow-up material to new converts.

UFA, BELORUSSIA

TOP: The stadium in Novosibirsk was filled to more than capac   th crowds of up to 39,000 breaking all of the stadium's records for attendance.
MIDDLE: Local volunteers unload tens of thousands of pieces of Christian literature.
BOTTOM: Team member and Swedish pastor, Christer Ihreborg, was almost pulled into the crowd by people anxious to get their first copy of the Bible.

NOVOSIBIRSK, RUSSIA

Left: Here I am with Vasco. He had never walked but his mother bought him a new pair of shoes to come to the crusade in faith that he would be healed. What a joy to see him run around the platform, healed by Jesus.

Above: 40,000 people stood for several hours in the pouring rain in anticipation of the start of the crusade. By the second night 70,000 had gathered.

Right: An elderly gentleman holds his glasses in his hands as he shows how Jesus healed his eyes.

PLOVDIV, BULGARIA

Above: The all-time attendance record was broken as 58,000 filled the National Stadium Alma Ata, Kazakhstan.

Above and Right: This Kazakh grandma got real excited when her blind eyes were open by Jesus. She could hardly contain herself!

ALMA ATA, KAZAKHSTAN

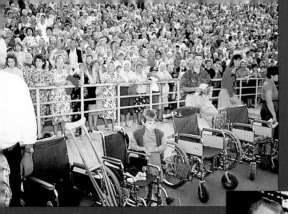

Left: Wheelchairs sit empty during the crusade as their owners are healed by the power of God.

Right: Here my interpreter, Sasha Popov, is pushed around by the former occupant of this wheelchair. With great joy she wheeled him around the platform, rejoicing in what Jesus had done!

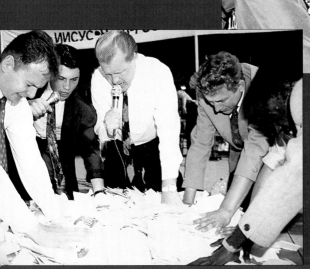

Left: Reis James, local church leaders and I pray over the hundreds of prayer requests that came in during each service.

VOLGOGRAD, RUSSIA

Above Left: A woman healed of paralysis holds her crutches high and dances for joy.
Above Right: A man healed of blindness counts my fingers to demonstrate.
Below: In Riga, Latvia this excited woman shows how she has been healed by Jesus.

"I SAW JESUS!"

"After Semipalatinsk, we moved to another Kazakh city, Karaganda, which had played a vital role in the Soviet space program for years, and until recently was a high security, 'closed' city. This city, Kazakhstan's second largest, prided itself for its technology and intelligence.

"Knowing this, I was dumbfounded to hear Mayor Chiamirden Urazalinov commission me to drive sin and iniquity from his city! 'God cannot bless sin, and we desperately need His blessing,' the mayor told me.

"With very little advertising, we started in the main stadium (donated by the mayor,) with only eight hundred people. The first night was uneasy, to say the least; a large stadium with only eight hundred people, many reporters, and the Chief Minister of Public Health for the province, Dr. Nikolei Kalpan, who was sent to verify any healings.

"The Holy Spirit took advantage of the opportunity! A young boy, Andre Barinova, born without an ear drum, began to hear! God performed a creative miracle.

"Two children, Sava Kalpakidi and Gorti, both who were completely paralysed down one side of their bodies since birth, were instantaneously and completely healed by Jesus power. From the very first night people began discarding canes and crutches.

"The following day at a press conference, the reporters were so astounded they sat in stunned silence! Only one dared ask me anything.

"Even Dr. Kalpan was amazed, and on a radio talk show he confessed, 'I am a medical doctor, I don't know how this is happening, or why it is happening, but it is happening; people are receiving miracles!' To further frustrate the matter, Dr. Kalpan's Jewish father was healed as well!

"For three consecutive nights the crowd kept growing until over twenty thousand had gathered. The people of Karaganda openly wept as they witnessed tokens of God's love for them. Most had assumed that God had only judgement and wrath accumulated for them.

"Mariana had consulted witches to seek healing for eye problems resulting from an accident. With tears and a sobs she testified that there was no power in the occult, only in Jesus!

"Perhaps the most touching miracle was that of a young boy born deaf and dumb. After mass prayer, he began to guard his ears from the invading noise of our sound system. His mother, who was overcome with gratitude, wept uncontrollably as I knelt down and whispered into the boys ear 'mamma.' His little voice, softly but definitely repeated 'mamma.' The mother was almost in need of healing herself as for the first time she heard her own child call her, 'mamma.' The final night we were to get more of the same.

"At 3:00 o'clock in the afternoon a lady suffering from heart failure was sped away to the hospital by ambulance. On hearing that the doctors could do nothing for her, she demanded to be taken to our crusade. After a lengthy, heated discussion the woman was transported to the stadium. Jesus rewarded the dear woman's faith and perseverance as she danced on the platform!

"The last lady to testify was an old Kazakh lady who had been totally blind for several years. After the mass prayer her eyes grew warm, and, a white sticky fluid poured into her handkerchief. When she finished wiping her eyes, she shrieked as she could see perfectly!

"Seeing the overwhelming response and having announced the starting of a new church, we secured the local skating arena for the follow-up services. Over four thousand people showed up.

"At the end of the teaching service, there was a great shrieking and commotion in the back as a rather large woman forced her way through the crowd. She ran onto the platform and wrestled the microphone from my hands to began telling her story: 'I have been crippled for twenty years. I was an invalid. I had no one to carry me to the stadium during the crusade. I live very close to this arena. I convinced my friends to carry me here. As I laid in the back all of a sudden I saw Jesus! The next thing I knew, I was standing and walking. Jesus had healed me!

"Her simple testimony adequately expresses the effect of the Karaganda crusade: 'I saw Jesus!' Where atheism and godless communism had clouded people's desire for God and reality; where generations have suffered under oppression and pain. Jesus showed Himself alive in all His love and power!"

10

GOD'S FIRE IN SIBERIA

By Pastor Vitali Maksymink, Hope Church,
Novrosibirsk, Russia.

Siberia! Cold and boundless! Long ago there were only forests and impassable waters in this cold Russian province. Later, in the times of Stalin, revolutionaries were sent here. Today the "red" blinders have fallen from the peoples' eyes and the lies of Bolshevism have left the country economically, ecologically and spiritually bare. Old sicknesses, which were never discussed have been disclosed and as never before our country needs spiritual help.

In July 1991 five young people started a church, which they simply called "Hope," of which I became the pastor. Within a short time thirteen Siberians accepted Christ and were baptized in water. The church grew and its activities broadened. Since the beginning the church gathered in a special 500 seat hall at the "October Revolution Cultural House." During the evil years of Communism this was known as the "House of Stalin."

The average age of our church membership is twenty-six and from the beginning it has been known for the powerful, lively and joyful worship to God.

When Peter Youngren came to visit our city, the Siberians warmly welcomed him. His dynamic sermons could be summarized in the words of John:

"For God so loved the world that He gave His only begotten Son, that whoever believes in Him should not perish but have everlasting life." [1]

The Gospel was truly fulfilled in our midst: the blind saw, the deaf heard, and the lame walked. There was widespread advertising and tens of thousands were able to see the truth of the advertisements and were convinced that there were indeed verified healings taking place.

Even before the crusade started the entire city and surrounding suburbs knew of the coming event. No sports event or entertainment had ever elicted such a response in the stadium. This is not just my subjective opinion, but this has been confirmed by the stadium director, a person who is certainly not very religious.

During the four-day crusade all sections of the stadium were filled. People came early to occupy the seats closest to the platform. Not only were the stands filled but, people stood on the grass in front of the platform.

The anointed preaching was heard by people of all ages and lifestyles from the most humble Christian believer to the greatest rebel in the city. The crowd included small children, many sick people, as well as many elderly. People were seen on crutches, wheelchairs and stretchers in various parts of the stadium. Everyone listened to the preaching with great attention and prayed the prayer of repentance, calling on the name of Jesus Christ.

As we were looking at the crowd, we could sense the supernatural lifegiving power of God descending on the people.

Each evening service began with joyful praises. An assistant to Pastor Youngren, Anthony Greco, helped out by preparing the people for the sermon. Peter Youngren's preaching was focused on the accomplishment of Jesus Christ at Calvary.

Thousands of people hungrily accepted the good news. Even those who were highly educated and attending had to confirm that indeed spiritual changes cause physical changes. After the prayer of repentance and salvation when everybody prayed along, there was time for a prayer for the sick. As the Bible says:

> *"The prayer of faith will heal the sick and the Lord will raise him up.... Confess your trespasses to one another, and pray for one another, that you may be healed. The effective, fervent prayer of a righteous man avails much."* [2]

The celebration ended with a demonstration of God's great love. With understandable joy and amazement people who had been sick began to move their paralysed arms and legs, seemingly unable to believe what they were seeing with their own eyes.

The Holy Spirit urged the people to act with individuality in believing God. This kind of independent action has been forgotten for a long time, due to the influence of Communism. Now people were hugging and kissing, overwhelmed with joy. Others were throwing down crutches which were no longer needed.

I'll never forget the immeasurable joy of the mother whose son stepped out of a wheelchair, or the joy of a son whose elderly mother had been blind and now received her sight. The word spoken by the prophet Isaiah seven hundred years before the coming of Jesus: *"Himself took our infirmities and bore our sicknesses,"*[5] was being fulfilled before our very eyes.

In spite of Peter Youngren's simple preaching explaining the Gospel, the ushers had to continually respond to a mountain of questions from the crowd. They were wondering, "Who is Jesus Christ?" "Who is Peter Youngren?" "Where does healing come from?" etc.

This really shows the lack of spiritual understanding. The ushers kept reinforcing the word that was preached from the platform, that Jesus is the healer and that faith in His word gets the job done.

The ushers also helped those who received their healing to make their way to the platform to testify. One after the other came to the microphone literally radiating with joy over the mercy of God on their lives.

One elderly lady of about seventy years old was jumping up and down happily and in amazement and was asking everybody where could she throw her crutches because she didn't need to bring them home with her.

An Afghan grandfather stood on the platform with thick

glasses and a hearing aid in his hand, and as the pastor whispered words in his ear he repeated them perfectly. I'll never forget a young woman overcome with tears. She had brought her five year old boy to the meeting. From early childhood he had been paralysed and was now standing on his own feet for the first time. Another little boy had a growth the size of a fist on his neck and now it had disappeared.

It's hard to know who was experiencing the greatest joy: the healed, their families, Pastor Peter Youngren, myself or the stadium full of people.

The word "hallelujah" continually echoed through the air. The final service was a wonderful sight as people, recognizing the great occasion at hand, had dressed up in their very best clothes.

An attractive young girl, Marie, who was standing somewhat shyly in the background, had her thick glasses in her hand. When we asked her what had happened, she responded, "I've been very near-sighted, and had to wear these terribly thick glasses for many years. Today a new world has opened up to me. I don't believe it, I can't believe it and yet I do believe it, because I can see, I can see."

Masha, a young girl who had been severely impaired in her eyesight, proved she had regained her ability to read by quoting the words on the illuminated billboard almost 500 metres away.

We give all the glory to the Lord Jesus forever and ever for the things He has done; for the way He has chosen to reveal His power to the city of Novosibirsk.

Hundreds and hundreds received their healings while at

the same time there were those who didn't seemingly receive any physical change. Even at that we have to remember the words of Jesus Christ saying,

"According to your faith let it be to you." [3]

It was also made very clear to the people that it is not sufficient just to see an external manifestation of God's power, but it is necessary for each person to receive God's power into their life and to grow in faith daily and continue to walk in a lifestyle of holiness.

Peter Youngren would return as "souvenirs" the crutches, canes, glasses and hearing aids to those who had been healed. Everyone in the crowd received a New Testament to take home with them. Even though the service would end at a certain time, the crowd would not disperse till much later. They would stay around for several hours sharing with others what they had received both physically and spiritually.

The effects of this Gospel festival will be long felt in the city and it will be a continuous topic of discussion for many. Recently, even city leaders, who are atheists were forced to acknowledge that the Gospel festival changed our city. Jesus is attracting the attention of people everywhere and is softening their hearts.

I am reminded of the words of Jesus, *"I have come that they may have life, and that they may have it more abundantly."* [4]

1   John 3:16
2   James 5:16
3   Matthew 9:29
4   John 10:10

11

UPLIFT IN UFA

God has always been a multiplier! It was never His intention that the Gospel would be confined. From the very beginning He raised the sights of those 12, those 120 and those 500 to whom He spoke before His ascension that the church had to be a world-embracing movement.

It cannot stop!

Every ministry has an obligation to multiply itself.

> *"And the things that you have heard from me among many witnesses, commit these to faithful men who will be able to teach others also."* [1]

Here are four generations of disciples of Jesus. First Paul, then Timothy, thirdly, faithful men and finally "others also."

One of the greatest joys in my life has been to be able to impart the vision God has given me to others. One of the finest co-workers I've ever had is Reis James from Lewiston, New York. Truth is caught more than taught and Reis and Joanne James have caught something in their spirit which has made them into people of prayer, commitment and dedication.

In 1987 Reis travelled with me and we ministered to tens of thousands of people in Moslem Pakistan. Our hotel rooms were on the same floor and I remember often coming off the elevator on our floor and even though Reis' room was located far away from the elevator landing, I could hear him speaking in tongues and interceding for the crusade the minute I stepped off the elevator.

Reis had spoken in churches and crusades for several years, however the large crusade forum when you are able to shake a whole city through a week of meetings was fairly new to him when he went to the Russian city of Ufa.

As he arrived in the city he found that the organization and the preparations for the crusade were, to say the least, in a mess. Yet it was evident that God had supernaturally been preparing the way for a successful outreach that would not only bear fruit, but that would bear fruit that would remain. I'll let him tell the story.

WORD OF KNOWLEDGE

"Our first stop was at the television and radio station in Ufa. Prior to our arrival, God had given us a word of knowledge (supernatural impartation of knowledge known only to God, not to man,) about an employee at the station, who had one leg shorter than the other. The word was that God would grow his leg out through the prayer of faith and by this miracle a door of opportunity would open for us to preach on television. When we arrived at the station, I asked if there was an employee who had one leg shorter then the other.

"Well, it so happened that there was and he was sitting

right behind us. We asked the fellow employees to come over and watch as Jesus would perform a miracle.

"After giving him a brief explanation that we were not healers, but that Jesus is the healer, we prayed; and could you ever see the joy in the man's face as his leg was lengthened to its proper size.

"He described to his fellow employees the warm feeling that he felt going through his body. The employees of the station were amazed by the power of God and asked us to go on television and tell people about Jesus' great love plan and His miracle power for everyone.

"We showed the 29 minute miracle video that has been produced based on Peter Youngren's crusades in the Eastern European block. This has been shown on station after station to prepare people for the actual crusade. After the video presentation, I was given an additional 15 minutes free air time to just preach and explain more about the video and what the person of Jesus is all about.

"Though organizationally almost nothing of what we usually have done before the crusade had actually been accomplished, God used the showing of this telecast so that a thousand people showed up at the crusade ground the day before the actual crusade was announced looking for this miracle Jesus. Well, we invited them to come back for the opening night and in that first service 8,000 people had gathered at central square in Ufa, wondering when the miracles would begin to take place.

"They asked questions typical of 'unchurched' people: 'Where do we stand?' or 'Where do we have to sign our name to get in on this?' They obviously had no idea how a Gospel meeting was usually conducted. These people were hungry for spiritual realities. We saw the love of God in action as people just simply responded to God's message of salvation.

"After preaching I asked for those who would like to receive Jesus as their personal Lord and Saviour and repent of sin, and as far as I could see every one of the 8,000 people eagerly raised their hand indicating that they wanted to be born again.

"It was such a moving sight, one that you don't easily forget. After the prayer of repentance, I announced to the people that we were now ready to pray for the sick. Well, it seemed that nearly everyone had a physical need.

"Just as we have seen it done in crusades all over the world, we just prayed a mass prayer believing that the Holy Spirit would move and that faith would rise and that they would indeed receive healing. They were not to be disappointed! We continued the second night and again, there were more miracles.

"By the third day we didn't know what to expect. The weather had suddenly turned bad. It was raining, but when we arrived at the crusade we saw something very beautiful: 25,000 people standing in the rain with umbrellas of every color that you can imagine. They were not going to let a little rain stop them from getting what they needed from Jesus. We were told that people had been lining up for over two hours just to be sure that they wouldn't miss out. Well, with faith like that you know that miracles are going to happen.

"What a night as paralytics walked, the blind saw, deaf

heard and many people were healed in the name of Jesus. By the fifth and final night 45,000 people had gathered in that open field. The name of Jesus was spreading throughout the city. His name was on everyone's lips and He was impacting and changing lives.

"A man from a Moslem background particularly stands out in my memory from that last service. He had broken his back months ago and had suffered with severe pain, not having a single day without pain since the accident. Well, he came to the platform and testified to the whole crowd that he was no longer Moslem, that he had accepted Jesus and that Jesus had healed his injured back. At the end of his testimony he said 'I only regret that I didn't come to these meetings sooner. Please everyone in the crowd, I encourage you to accept Jesus as you Lord and Saviour.' What a miracle!

"Our Pastor, Peter Youngren, continually stresses that we must not just conduct a healing crusade, but must impart truth and love and faith into the hearts of local pastors and local churches so that there will be a strong ministry continued.

"After the crusade we continued with three days of follow-up meetings to give people a deeper foundation. So many people showed up we had to rent a second auditorium and have the sound piped into the additional space. There were people in the aisles, on the floor, on the stage and every spot in between; in hallways, everywhere. Hundreds of people were baptized in water and we thank God for what He is doing in Russia."

What a tremendous testimony by Reis James.

When new churches like this are birthed, or young

churches receive a major growth spurt like the ones described in this book, we continue to love and bless and reach out to the new people.

Throughout the winter months when mass crusades are impossible because of the weather conditions, apostolic church planting teams are visiting Russia and Eastern Europe every month. The things we have received must be passed on to other faithful people, who in their turn are able to pass it on.

1   II Timothy 2:2

12

EXPERIENCES OF A MIRACLE RECORDER

By Vivian Fransson

From time to time I've heard Peter Youngren talk about how one, or often, several miracle recorders are on the platform to record the diagnosis of sicknesses and report on miracles which have occurred. Well in September 1992 it was my turn. It was my first trip to the Russian city of Volgograd. Our experience started as we boarded AEROFLOT, the Russian airline.

To be totally honest, I thought with some humor that if I don't make it to Russia, I'm sure that I'll make it to heaven. The plane had seen better days. My husband's chair back was not functional, so he spent the trip leaning on the kneecaps of the passenger behind him. To be really sure, I'd laid hands on the plane before boarding and pleaded the protection of the blood of Jesus.

Once in Moscow, more than an hour passed before we got our suitcases. People were pushing and shoving everywhere. I was to say the least irritated, thinking to myself, "Vivian, welcome on your first missionary journey and welcome to reality?"

We had three hours to catch our next plane and about 60 miles to the domestic airport. Once we got our suitcases less than two hours remained. After customs, we encountered our next trial: a group of taxi drivers looking for customers.

Somewhat naive and stressed out, we were easy prey for the "taxi mafia," and they sure took advantage of it. Our driver drove like a man possessed, but we actually made it to the domestic airport and I had to confess that it was worth the price.

No one spoke English in the narrow and very shabby domestic terminal. Everything was in Russian, but God was with us. All of a sudden behind us there appeared an African student, who spoke English and was also on his way to Volgograd. He helped us and showed us the right gate.

Once in Volgograd no one was there to meet us. My husband and I were forlorn-looking individuals in the middle of a very windy airport terminal in the middle of the night. Once again the African student helped us find the city and a hotel. The next day the crusade would start.

So far, not much has gone according to calculations, but I understood God wanted something special in this city. Volgograd was once called Stalingrad and it is under this name that the city is famous, for it was here that the Russian army defeated one quarter of the Nazi forces on the eastern front in the largest battle of the Second World War. I knew that God wanted to demonstrate His power over our enemy Satan in this vast city of over a million people.

In the center of the city on a hill there is a statue almost 175 feet high, of a woman with a drawn sword. It is in memory of the great battle fought. This was a reminder to me that God wanted something similar to happen in the spirit realm. He wanted to drive out the spiritual oppression and set the people in liberty through Jesus. He wanted to drive out sickness and sin and see people saved by the tens of thousands.

And that's what really happened. The crusade was scheduled for four days. Up to a couple of days before the crusade there was no advertising and it looked like we may have to preach to an empty stadium. As a result, the first night we only had four thousand people present, but the crowd grew from night to night as the rumors spread of the miracles. By the last night, twenty six thousand people had gathered.

It was incredible to see the response of the people. It was like Peter was preaching straight into a vacuum; to people seemingly void of any knowledge of God. They just received.

Being from a Norwegian background, known to be somewhat conservative, it was a little difficult for me to grasp what was happening at first. We have been so indoctrinated in Western Europe to doubt the miraculous, that when we see simple faith in action it's almost hard to believe what you're seeing.

Sitting on the platform I saw about 90 per cent of the people raise their hands when the invitation was given to receive Jesus. My brain could hardly register that this was really happening. Yet, indeed it was. This was reality.

I've attended two years of Bible School, studied about the healing power of Jesus, and in my heart I believed miracles are for today, yet I almost felt embarrassed when I saw how, in such simple faith, the people were receiving the miraculous. God was doing lots and lots of miracles.

My task was to record what was happening. Sometimes so many things were happening so quickly that I had a difficult time to get all the facts. Anyhow I did my best and was able to record 57 fantastic testimonies. It feels like words cannot describe what my eyes saw.

I remember especially a woman, who had been crippled from a car accident. She was brought to the crusade by her sister. For six months she had been in a wheelchair and doctors had told her she would spend the rest of her life in that chair. Jesus healed her! Hallelujah!

Several children had been deaf and some who were blind received their hearing and sight. Several received both double and triple miracles. In other words they had several sicknesses and they all got healed.

I managed to record just the tip of the iceberg. People stood in a line-up to get to the platform to give their testimony and not everyone was allowed to share it, because we would have had to continue all night. As far as my rational thinking, what was happening was beyond comprehension, but the truth is, it was happening and I know it will continue.

If I will get the opportunity to take the same trip again: suffer through AEROFLOT, the "taxi mafia," the uncertainty of an empty airport terminal in the middle of the night and then see everything God did, I wouldn't hesitate. It's worth it many times over. God didn't just do miracles in Russian hearts but also in mine. Finally, it has been planted deep in my spirit that

He is a God of miracles.

Excerpts from Vivian's diary of miracles:

• Thursday, September 3 - Sasha, a six year old boy who was born deaf received healing and hears perfectly.

• Thursday, September 3 - Middle-aged woman who has been unable to walk at all for seven years has been healed and is now walking freely.

• Thursday, September 3 - Maiva has been crippled for ten years; now she's able to bend, move, do everything.

• Thursday, September 3 - Natasha, a young woman, has not been able to walk for three years and is walking and running.

• Thursday, September 3 - An elderly man who has been totally blind in his left eye since childhood and blind for a long time in his other eye, is now seeing everything perfectly.

• Thursday, September 3 - Luba, who has been deaf for fourteen years, is now able to hear.

• Friday, September 4 - Natalja, who has been deaf for twenty years, has received her hearing.

• Friday, September 4 - Anja has been paralysed by a stroke down her right leg since one year ago. She is now free.

• Friday, September 4 - Igor, a young boy who has

been deaf and dumb for two years, has been healed. His grandmother has brought him and she is rejoicing exceedingly.

• Friday, September 4 - A young man has had two tumors on his knees for the last two years about the size of plums. Instantly they have vanished.

• Saturday, September 5 - Tamara, who arrived at the stadium in a wheelchair, said she has not been able to walk since 1987. Now she is walking around rejoicing pushing her wheelchair.

• Saturday, September 5 - Kazakhsim, has been healed from stuttering that he suffered with for four years.

• Sunday, September 6 - A woman who has been blind since 1947 receives her sight.

• Sunday, September 6 - Paval, who has been crippled in his right leg has received healing.

• Sunday, September 6 - Ina, was in a car accident six months ago and has since been paralysed. Now she is walking and running.

13

THE GREAT HARVEST

Throughout church history there have been many times of spiritual harvest or revival, but in the Gospel of Matthew, Jesus speaks about "the harvest." This refers to a spiritual harvest at the end of time that will be greater than any other in magnitude.

> *"The field is the world, the good seeds are the sons of the kingdom, but the tares are the sons of the wicked one. The enemy who sowed them is the devil, the harvest is the end of the age, and the reapers are the angels."* [1]

Later on Jesus speaks about the end of the world and of this great harvest when he compares it with a large net cast into the sea.

> *"Again, the kingdom of heaven is like a dragnet that was cast into the sea and gathered some of every kind, which, when it was full, they drew to shore; and they sat down and gathered the good into vessels, but threw the bad away. So it will be at the end of the age. The angels will come forth, separate the wicked from among the just."* [2]

God's plan for the end of the world is a 'catch of fish,' 'people of every kind.' The net that is drawn to shore will be full. Full of people from every ethnic group.

There are scriptures which indicate that there will be more people in heaven then in hell.

> *"But the free gift is not like the offense. For if by the one man's offense many died, much more the grace of God and the gift by the grace of the one Man, Jesus Christ, abounded to many."* [3]

Yes, billions have been affected by Adam's sin and so also billions can be affected by the grace of Jesus.

> *"For as by one man's disobedience many were made sinners, so also by one Man's obedience many will be made righteous."* [4]

Adam's disobedience had far reaching effect; so Jesus' obedience will also reach far.

> *"After these things I looked, and behold, a great multitude which no one could number, of all nations, tribes, peoples, and tongues, standing before the throne and before the Lamb, clothed with white robes, with palm branches in their hands, and crying out with a loud voice, saying, 'Salvation belongs to our God who sits on the throne, and to the Lamb!'"* [5]

Heaven will be full of people, a crowd that "no one" can number.

Two thousand years ago the earth's population was approximately 250,000,000, less than the population of the United States today. By 1850 one billion populated the world. From Adam it took almost six thousand years for the earth's population to reach one billion. By 1930 two billion populated our planet. By 1988 the population had reached five billion. Today we are at five and a half billion inhabitants. The fifth billion took only ten years from 1978 to 1988, while the first billion took almost six thousand years.

This is called "population explosion." Should the return of Jesus tarry, many futurologists estimate that the earth's population by the year 2025 A.D. will be close to fifteen billion individuals. This is all staggering, but it helps us to understand Jesus' prophetic statement that 'the harvest' was to come at the 'end of time.' There has never been a more opportune time for a great harvest of people than today.

How will the Church react to and cope with these changes in history? If we continue to move at our present speed and level of commitment I'm afraid we may fail.

My faith, however, is not in what has happened in the past, but in God's promise that a generation will arise and get the job done.

Two years ago, at the start of Word of Life Church in St. Catharines, God gave us a vision which I believe is also applicable to the Church at large. Let the vision God gave us touch you and then seek God for the precise vision He has for you. Remember that God's individual vision for you will fit in, like the piece of a puzzle, with God's overall plan for this generation.

The vision is four-fold.

1. <u>To raise up a people totally dedicated to Jesus</u>

At the present level of dedication we will continue to see the same results we have seen in the past. It takes effort to raise up a people. Churchgoers do not automatically become dedicated by hearing sermons and prayers. They must be raised up, trained, equipped and given role models of people, who themselves are sold out to Jesus. The generation of people that will get the job done must be totally dedicated to the person of Jesus. Something beyond good intention and nice desires must be deposited in our spirit. That something is a great sense of call. It's fire from heaven; fire in your bones.

I am not writing this as a rebuke of past generations. Thank God for the tears, the labour, and the love that have moved the Gospel message forward in the past. However, we must recognize we are in a generational 'shift.'

When Moses died, God spoke to Joshua the son of Nun,

> *"Now therefore, arise, go over this Jordan,*
> *you and all this people, to the land which I am*
> *giving to them; the children of Israel."* [6]

King David also represented a new generation of anointing.

Elisha pressed in for a 'double portion,' refusing to settle for the status quo. He desired more of God's manifested power and fire in his life than even Elijah, his mentor.

We are coming into a time period when a generation is being raised up to do the works of Jesus. One man can never do it. We need thousands of men and women of God to shake cities for God.

This involves millions of individual believers, who will live their lives in total dedication to see revival in their own local churches, cities, nations and the world. This is a people whose time, finances, energies, and talents are dedicated to the kingdom of God and to the success principles in that kingdom, rather than success in the world's system.

2. To tear down spiritual strongholds

These strongholds can be found not only in society at large, but in the Church. Many believers have learned to settle for second best. When Paul and his team entered a city their mentality was clear, it was one of "taking over."

There is a spirit of defeatism that can easily creep into any church setting. One easily gets accustomed to little growth, a little excitement, a few answers to prayer and little spiritual energy. It is easy to settle within the four walls of the sanctuary. It takes a 'breakthrough anointing' to tear down such a stronghold of defeatism.

The purpose of this chapter is not to elaborate on all the strongholds of society. Materialism, New Age philosophy and Secular Humanism are only a few of the ones that could be mentioned. It takes people with understanding of the times and breakthrough anointing to operate successfully in a world like ours. The temptation will always be to cave in, to lower one's expectations in order to adjust to society.

3. To lay a Word based foundation

The Great Commission is not just to win souls, but to

teach nations. In Kazakhstan, one of the educational leaders said to us, "We know now that Communism was a colossal mistake. Our three hundred years of Moslem history has been removed and no one remembers our Christian heritage from four hundred years back. Can you teach us how to live?"

This challenge is for individuals, who themselves have laid a Word based foundation in their lives. You cannot take others where you have not been yourselves. Christ's commission to the Church still stands; to "teach nations."

We do more than just conduct crusades and soul winning seminars, though these may be the most noticeable aspect of our work. Teams are continually going out conducting teaching seminars for leaders, seminars to strengthen local churches, and follow-up endeavors to train new believers.

A half-hearted, 'hit and miss' approach will not get the job done. The church has to mobilize like an army. Pastors and local churches in America must embrace the world and stand shoulder to shoulder together bringing in the spiritual harvest.

4. <u>To commission and equip believers</u>

Every word in this fourth point in our vision carries a significance. People are to be "commissioned" out of a local church. Paul and Barnabas were sent out of the Church in Antioch.[7] After their missionary journey they reported back to that same local church.

There is a vast difference between just going out or being 'sent' out. For years, because of lack of 'world vision' and zeal, ministries have gone out hoping and believing for support and help. Of course this has brought results, but God has a better way.

People who are sent out with the support of a strong local church that is already moving in a breakthrough anointing, carry this anointing into the spiritual harvest field.

One doesn't send a soldier to battle without equipment. Proper training in doing the works of Jesus is a must. Often Bible Schools have given people the ability to discuss theology fluently and intelligently; while they have imparted little understanding in how to deal with demonic forces that operate in nations, cities and individuals. Bible Colleges must emphasize not only academic excellence, but also training in how to operate in the gifts of the Spirit, how to intercede successfully and how to tear down demonic strongholds. People must learn how to have breakthroughs in regional, as well as in personal matters.

It is in this context that we must understand and see the teaching on prosperity that has come to the church over the last ten years. Prosperity, in the Bible, always came to God's people for the express purpose of accomplishing God's plan. Personal comfort is wonderful, but it must never be one's motivation in living. We believe in and teach prosperity so that God's covenant will be established. Simultaneously, with God raising up an army of believers willing to move across the earth to preach and lay hands on the sick, God also raises up an army of people with the ability and faith to finance God's end time program.

There have been many revivals and reformations throughout church history. Already in this century, hundreds of millions have been swept into the kingdom of God.

However, Jesus spoke of "the harvest," the harvest of all harvests. I believe we are on the threshold of it.

It will come through a people, who have received fire from heaven. A mere experience with God is not sufficient. Many have had experiences, like weeping in God's presence, being moved by a sermon, or even seeing a vision.

Of course, experiences are valuable, but the harvest field of billions of lost souls will be reached by a people, who have gone beyond the "point of spiritual experiences." It will be a people who have given their lives wholly to Jesus, the Lord of the harvest.

The Lordship of Jesus demands everything, and a new breed of disciples of Jesus are being raised up, who are willing to pay that price.

The fire of God keeps burning. It is not temporary. It is the result of a life dedicated to Jesus. Let the fire touch your life.

1   Matthew 13:38-39
2   Matthew 13:47-49
3   Romans 5:15
4   Romans 5:19
5   Revelation 7:9-10
6   Joshua 1:2
7   Acts 13:1-2

EQUIPPING

YOU

TO SHAKE YOUR

WORLD

WORLD IMPACT BIBLE INSTITUTE

W.I.B.I. is the unique training facility founded by Peter Youngren to equip people to make a difference in their city, country and the world. Whether your desire is to be a dynamic believer, a world missionary or a pastor, W.I.B.I. is the place for you!
Full two year Ministerial Program and one year Christian Leadership Program.
Send for your FREE information packet today!

- - - - - - - - - - - - - - - - - -

Please rush me more info. about W.I.B.I.!

Name:_____

Address:_____

City: _____

Prov./State: _____

Code: _____

Mail to: The Registrar
World Impact Bible Institute
P.O. Box 968
St. Catharines, ON
L2R 6Z4
or call (416) 646-0970

Visit...
WORD OF LIFE CHURCH

oin Pastor Peter Youngren
nd the congregation of
Vord of Life Church for a
fe-changing experience of
reakthrough. Word of Life
as been raised up by God
o be a strong local church
n the Niagara Peninsula
nd a centre for spiritual
efreshing for believers
om around the world.
Vhether attending a regular
ervice or coming for a
pecial conference, your
xperience at Word of Life
sure to be exciting and
ewarding! Come,
xperience Jesus at Word of
ife!

POWER-PACKED CONFERENCESS

- CANADA CAMPMEETING

- YOUTH CONFERENCES

- WORSHIP EXPLOSIONS

- TAKE IT BY FORCE

- MEN'S SEMINARS

...and many others.

EXPERIENCE JESUS

Please send me more information about Word of Life!

ame: _____

ddress: _____

ty: _____

ov./State: _____

de: _____

Send to: WORD OF LIFE CHURCH
P.O. Box 968
St. Catharines, ON
L2R 6Z4
or call (416) 646-0970